# The Hebrides
# in old picture postcards

by
Francis Thompson

European Library – Zaltbommel/Netherlands

GB ISBN 90 288 4784 7 / CIP

© 1989 European Library  –  Zaltbommel/Netherlands

No part of this book may be reproduced in any form, by print, photoprint, microfilm or any other means without written permission from the publisher.

# INTRODUCTION

The islands which comprise the Outer Hebrides (Lewis, Harris, North Uist, Benbecula, South Uist, Barra, and their various satellite islands) have been known to the recorders of ancient history for at least two thousand years. There is, however, much visible evidence to indicate that the islands were inhabited for at least two millenia before the advent of the Christian era. The most outstanding memorial to the Hebrideans of 4,000 years ago is to be seen at Callanish, where a rough circle of standing stones, dated to c. 1900 B.C., offers a mute but impressive witness to the long distant past. The Callanish Stones are rated second only to those at Stonehenge, in the south of England, with which they are contemporary, and also with the stones at Carnac, in France.

Although today the islands of the Hebrides are now largely covered with peat, it was not the case about 2,500 years ago. Then, a milder climate nourished trees and shrubs, the remains of which are often uncovered when the peat is dug out for fuel, a practice which is both time-honoured and very much in evidence today. Particularly along the western seaboard, facing the Atlantic, the remains of tree trunks can be seen under the sea. The climate then changed to become a wetter, colder and less hospitable environment and a blanket of peat began to grow which now covers what might be left of Hebridean prehistory.

To what race the first Hebrideans belonged is still a matter for conjecture. However, the fact that carved stones have been found in the Hebrides, similar to the Pictish carved stones found on the Scottish mainland, leads one to surmise that the islanders were, to a large extent, of that ancient race who finally became extinct c. 800 A.D., leaving nothing but a few placenames from their language and the carved monuments as a memorial to their remarkable culture and artistry.

In the 3rd century A.D., the Gaelic-speaking Scots came over to Scotland from Ireland, and their spread throughout the western seaboard took them inevitably to the Outer Hebrides. This movement of the Gaels was given an impetus when St. Columba, a priest-king from Ireland, landed on the island of Iona in 563 to set up the foundations of the Celtic Church. His missionaries took the word of the Gospel to the Hebrides.

During the 8th century, the sea-faring Vikings started their colonisation of these islands. They founded many of the clan families whose surnames are with us today: MacLeod, MacIver, Morrison, MacAulay, MacNeil, MacDonald. Though the Norsemen occupied the islands for nearly four centuries, before they were expelled from Scotland in 1263, they failed to implant a Norse culture and language over the residual and indigenous Gaelic tongue. That is... apart from the placenames of the islands. Virtually all placenames found on the seaboard are of Norse origin, while the names of topographical features inland are mostly Gaelic.

Gaelic is now the indigenous language of the Hebrides and belongs to the family of Celtic languages which includes Irish Gaelic, Welsh, Cornish, Breton and Manx. Despite the dominance of English, over 90 percent of the island population are native Gaelic speakers. Their Gaelic tradition was largely transmitted orally until the 18th century by 'sennachies'. These men and women were tradition-bearers whose memories were fantastic; some of the folk tales in the language took days to tell, all recited from memory without the aid of literature.

After the Norsemen left the Hebrides, the founder families of clans began to establish themselves in the islands. The island of Lewis was the territory of the MacAulays, the Morrisons (who were the heriditary 'breves' or judges) and the MacLeods, who eventually became the dominant clan. In the Uists, the MacDonalds of Clanranald held sway. And in Barra the Clan MacNeil held their island secure against all comers. The islands, being remote from the seat of Scottish government in Edinburgh, were thus ruled by the clan chiefs whose power was absolute. Their dynasties, however, were not to last. At the turn of the 16th century, the MacLeods lost control of Lewis to the Mackenzies of Seaforth, a Scottish mainland clan. Lewis was then sold in 1844 to Sir James Matheson, part of whose fortune was made in the opium trade in the Far East. The MacDonalds held on to the Uists until they became bankrupt in the 19th century, when they sold their estates to new owners. In the same period, the MacNeils sold Barra.

These changes in ownership created a great social upheaval. Most of the islands' population had no legal right to the land on which they lived. They were tenants 'at will' and as such could be dispossessed at a moment's notice. They were poor, lived in bad housing conditions and had little or no cash income. Thousands were forced to emigrate to Canada and America. Families were often broken up with parents being separated from their children. Many who tried to evade emigration were caught and thrown on board the waiting ships, bound and fettered.

It was not until 1886 that an Act of Parliament gave the crofters security of tenure and they were given restricted rights to cultivate their crofts. Since then the crofting system has provided the islands with a subsistence level of income. It has, however, also been instrumental in maintaining the islands' population and preserving the Gaelic language and its culture.

Much of the wealth of the Hebrides lies in the seas surrounding the islands, a wealth which has been exploited for well over a century by non-island interests, simply because the native islanders had no capital with which to buy fishing boats. Instead, they worked as crew members and were paid at the end of each fishing season. That might sound like an equitable system. In fact, the fishermen's families often had to go into debt for food and other necessities such as clothing, being subjected to the iniquitous 'truck' system. Often when a fishing season finished, the fisherman found that his wages totalled the debt. And if the fishing season was a poor one, he and his family had to carry the debt over to the next season.

The main fishing catch was herring, which virtually ruled the economy of the islands. Places like Stornoway and Castlebay during the middle years of last century were important herring stations and saw hundreds of fishing boats in their harbours, as some of the postcards in this book show. Women were often employed as herring gutters, with a skill with the knife which could gut a herring nearly every second. The herring were then packed tightly into barrels, separated by layers of rough salt. The barrels were then exported to Germany, and the Baltic states which now no longer exist, such as Latvia and Estonia.

If the sea's riches did not particularly benefit the islands, it was a blessing for Stornoway. Situated in a fine harbour, it has always looked to the sea for its prosperity. In its time Stornoway has been a major herring port, witnessed an era of successful shipbuilding and provided the world's shipping with both deckhands and captains. Many of the latter were captains of the fine sailing ships which last century raced half way round the world with cargoes of wool, tea and spices from the Far East. And not a few of them won the races to bring the first tea of the season into the port of London to command the highest prices.

The period covered by the postcards featured in this book is from c. 1880 to the 1930s. It was a period which saw slow change in housing conditions, the emergence of the world-famous Harris Tweed industry, the increase in sea traffic by ferries, the improvement in health and, indeed, the strengthening of the islanders' spirit of independence. Most of the postcards are from the author's personal collection, supplemented by material from the Lewis Museum and Stornoway Library, to whom the author is greatly indebted for their valuable help and co-operation.

Stornoway                                                                 Francis Thompson

1. Castlebay, Isle of Barra, just before the turn of the century. Prominent in the bay is Kismul Castle, still in its ruinous state after the structure caught fire in 1795. It was the stronghold of the clan MacNeil of Barra who, in mediaeval times, scoured the southern seas as pirates, even sailing as far south as Ireland for plunder. The fishing boats in the bay are wherries, characterised by the tall masts and massive brown sails. This picture was taken when the herring was still the king fish and Castlebay one of the major herring stations in Scotland. In very busy seasons it was said that one could walk across the decks of the boats to the isle of Vatersay in the distance. In the foreground are some of the 'black houses' which were so common throughout the Hebrides of the time. The more primitive types had no chimney, merely a hole in the roof through which the centrally-placed hearth dispersed the smoke from the peat fire. The walls were anything up to six feet (2m) thick. Notice the use of an old upturned boat as a roof on which fishing nets are draped to dry.

2. For a long time after the old Celtic Church, founded by St. Columba of Iona, was absorbed into the Church of Rome, the Hebrides were adherents to a primitive Catholic faith. This faith, however, was strong. Not a journey was undertaken, not a fire was kindled in the morning, not a cow was milked until a prayer had been uttered to invoke the spirit of Christ to bless the deed. For many centuries the religious integrity of the people was left to its own devices until 1652 when Father Dermit Duggan, of the Vincentian Fathers from Limerick in Ireland, was sent on a mission to revive the relics of the former faith. He and other priests of the Order of St. Francis found the people 'were so little instructed that they did not know how to make the sign of the Cross'. Slowly the formal structure of the Roman faith was resurrected. Today the church of Our Lady Star of the Sea, opened at Christmas 1889, stands a strong witness to the persistent ministrations of a long line of dedicated priests.

3. This view of Castlebay, taken from a departing ferry, dates from 1924. Kismul Castle is seen in its still ruinous state waiting until 1938 before a restoration programme was begun by a direct descendant of the MacNeils of Barra. The housing has improved in both style and grandeur. The pier, however, was for long in a parlous state, a wooden structure which barely managed to cope with the traffic it experienced when the ferry docked. All goods needed for the requirements of the Barra people had to be landed here. Any 'export' produce of Barra was also taken on board the ferry, such as lobsters, which had to be kept alive in boxes for their long journey to London Markets. While the fish is alive, its shell is air-tight. But once dead it decays quickly. Many consignments failed to make the journey, to the loss of the fisherman who had also to pay for the freight. In its heyday as a herring port, the population of Castlebay jumped from a couple of hundred to many thousands. By the time this picture was taken the herring industry had collapsed, leaving Castlebay a ghost town.

4. Barra has always depended for the necessities of life on the ferries, sailing from Oban on the Scottish mainland across the Sea of the Hebrides. Pictured here is the 'Lochearn', one of the fleet of ships of David MacBrayne Ltd. She was built in 1930 with a gross tonnage of 542. She could carry 400 passengers but also carried mails and cargo. Her ports of call were Mull, Coll, Tiree, Castlebay and Lochboisdale (South Uist). For her size she was extremely well fitted out with cabins, dining room, a smoking room and a lounge. In 1964 she was sold to Greek owners and renamed 'Amimoni'. Cars taken to Barra were placed on thick rope nets and then hoisted on and off the ship. The day on which the ferry arrived at Castlebay attracted both intending passengers and the locals, who crowded on the pier to watch the visitors to the island. The 'Lochearn' was only one of a long line of ferries, dating from the late decades of the 19th century, to serve the islands of the southern Hebrides. They were sturdy craft and seldom allowed bad weather to interfere with their sailings, though they were often storm-bound in port.

Kentangval. (Copyright.)

5. This picture of the tiny Barra crofting township of Kentagaval was taken c. 1890. It shows the characteristic features of many similar townships in the Hebrides. The thick walls consisted of two courses of rough stones up to 2m apart and filled in with earth and rubble. These supported the rafters which were then boarded over and covered with a straw thatch, which was secured by ropes weighted down by large stones. In the more primitive houses, the family lived in one end while the other end was used as a byre for a cow. One or two small windows were let into the walls, and fitted with a single sheet of glass. Sanitary conditions left much to be desired and were often a source of disease. At the date of this picture, crofters had only recently been given security of tenure through the Crofters Act of 1886. This Act gave them a few acres of poor ground, with a share in a larger area called 'common grazings' on which they could graze sheep and cattle. This offered the opportunity to glean the basic essentials for life, supplemented by fish and shell fish.

6. The island of Eriskay lies off the southern tip of South Uist. Its claim to historical fame is that it was on Prince Charlie's Strand that Prince Charles Edward Stuart first landed in July 1745 to seek support for a third Jacobite Rising to win back the British Crown for his father. He was later taken across The Minch to the Scottish mainland to raise the Standard of the Clans to begin the 'Forty-five Rebellion'. After some initial military successes against the English army, Prince Charles' insurrection was defeated at the Battle of Culloden, near Inverness, in April 1746. The island's name is derived from the Old Norse, 'Erik's Isle', echoing the days when the Vikings occupied the whole of the Hebrides. For its size, it has contributed much to the Gaelic tradition through the work of the priest, Fr. Allan MacDonald, who ministered to the people of Eriskay at the turn of the century. His collections of Gaelic words, folksongs and traditions comprise a rich vein which has been mined ever since by tradition collectors. One of these traditions is that when Prince Charles landed on Eriskay he dropped seeds of the convolulus, which still thrives.

7. Until the appearance of the motor car in the 1920s, the only means of carrying heavy loads was by pack pony. These ponies are of the Eriskay breed, which, as a class, is of great antiquity and the nearest to the race of horses that ran wild in Scotland before the arrival of man. They are docile animals, from 12 to 13 hands high and are now quite rare, with only about fifty animals now in existence. The foals are born black and grow up to take on a dark grey colour. On Eriskay they were used to carry baskets (or creels) of fish and peat cut from the moor, building materials, hay from the fields, and seaweed from the shore used to fertilise the ground before the planting of the staple food, potatoes.

8. A typical island family standing outside their home, just after the turn of the century. The rough-hewn boulders can be seen forming the outer course of the double-walled structure. The thatch, of straw and heather, is held down with ropes tied to stones to prevent the wind from tearing the covering away. Doors were never provided with locks. If privacy was needed, the door was simply closed and any visitor was required to knock. At the door of some old houses a large stone was provided as a seat for the visitor. The man wears the typical clothing of a fisherman, which was the main source of income for the people of Eriskay. The land being so poor, it could not yield sufficient to support a family's needs and so the Eriskay men became known for their skills as fishermen. Women, not tied down by families, often went to the Scottish fishing ports to earn a wage as herring gutters. At the time of this picture, a fisherman could count himself lucky to earn £8 in a season in hard cash. The large wooden tub seen to the left was used to soak wool before dyeing.

9. This is a very rare postcard taken shortly after the opening of the new Catholic Church on Eriskay in 1903. The prime mover behind the new building was Father Allan MacDonald, parish priest, who is seen in his robes on the path leading from the church. The funds for the building came from a number of sources, including gifts from a Russian Jew, born in Paris, who had heard that the former church had fallen into disrepair. All the Eriskay fishermen donated a day's fishing which yielded the best catch of the season worth £280. The Church has since been renovated and provided with an unusual altarpiece: the bow of the lifeboat from the aircraft carrier 'Hermes' which was washed overboard at St. Kilda and came ashore on South Uist. The altarpiece is reminiscent of the pulpit in the film 'Moby Dick' and eminently fitting for an island church. Father Allan, a noted folklorist, died in 1905 at the early age of 46, but is still remembered for his work on Eriskay eight decades after. The postcard is unusual for its all-Gaelic caption: 'Father Allan and the people after Mass on Eriskay.'

10. Lochboisdale, the 'capital' of South Uist at about the turn of the century. Its rather deserted appearance hardly echoes its former days when it had its share of the 'boom' years of the herring fishing industry. The fishing vessel berthed at the pier seems to long for her companions. The building with its gable facing the pier is the Lochboisdale Stores which, in the tradition of all Hebridean shops, sold anything 'from a pin to an anchor'. The rather imposing building in the centre of the picture was formerly a shop owned by a Mr. MacDougal. It is now a bank. However, true to the traditional long memory of the people of South Uist, it is still referred to as 'Buth MhicDoughaill', MacDougal's shop. The building on the left was erected as a Mission Church to cater for visiting fishermen who were not Catholics. According to a description of Lochboisdale in 1910, ships landing at Lochboisdale could buy 'barrels of biscuits, meal and potatoes'.

11. Another view of Lochboisdale. The imposing building on the right of the picture is Lochboisdale Hotel. For a time in 1880 the hotel housed a sub-post office when the Southern Hebrides Mail Service was introduced, and was empowered to datestamp letters 'Lochboisdale Pier'. The hotel was built in the 1870s to cater for the increasing number of tourists and sportsmen who found the Uists a perfect hunting ground for fishing and shooting. The pier was originally built by Sir John Powlett Orde, who bought the South Uist Estate from Lord MacDonald. The pier gave Lochboisdale not only status but presented an opportunity to build up its reputation as a trading station. Ferries began to call at the village with passengers and cargo, and take on board cattle from the island to the mainland of Scotland. The building to the left of the hotel was erected by an enterprising builder to offer some relaxation for visiting fishermen. It housed a restaurant, had ample space for dancing and was used as a library. It is now no longer part of the Lochboisdale scene. The two-storey building in the centre is now a shop and post office.

12. The post office at Howmore, South Uist around 1910, with its typical 'back house' construction converted to a commercial function. The post office at Howmore started life as a 'receiving house' in 1843, handling about thirty letters each week and producing an annual revenue of a little over £6. A relay of runners was employed by the post office to take letters to Lochmaddy in North Uist, three times weekly in summer and twice weekly in winter. The Howmore postmaster was both receiver and runner and had an annual joint salary of £13, which made him a relatively wealthy man. The original postmark of Howmore was simply the name between two straight lines. In 1880 Howmore came of age by being given an actual datestamp. By this time the 'runner' had been replaced by a horse-rider, who received 16 shillings a week for himself and 4 shillings for the upkeep of his horses. A proposal in 1884 for the horserider to be replaced by a mail coach was dropped because of the cost of its maintenance. The Howmore post office was finally closed in 1951.

13. Witnesses to the ancient and recent past of the Hebrides are scattered throughout the islands. Here the ruins (c. 1913) of the old church at Howmore, South Uist. The site is in fact a collection of buildings: two churches dedicated respectively to St. Mary and St. Columba, and two isolated chapels. The site itself dates from between the late 7th and 10th centuries A.D. By mediaeval times the buildings formed part of a monastery and college which had assumed a sufficiently high reputation for learning that it was visited by scholars not only from Scotland but also Europe. The structures are built of rubble in lime mortar and once had steep pitched roofs which were made of stone similar to the churches of the early Irish Christian period. In one of the buildings there is an armorial panel depicting a ship, a hand bearing a cross (the Red Hand of MacDonald), a castle, a lion and a bird. The site was partially dismantled after the Reformation in Scotland, in 1560, which reduced the Roman Catholic religion to second class status. One of the chapels was destroyed shortly before 1886.

14. If Eriskay saw the landing of Prince Charlie in July 1745, to restore the British Crown to Stuart heads, little did he think that in a little more than a year he would be in nearby South Uist, a fugitive from the English Army and with a price of £30,000 on his head. This picture, dated c. 1910, shows the ruins of Flora MacDonald's house (it was not her birthplace) near the township of Milton. A cairn has now been erected on the site to commemorate her part in helping Prince Charlie to escape to Skye. Flora was the daughter of Ronald MacDonald of Milton, who was a cadet of Clanranald (the MacDonalds who owned South Uist). The Prince, with a small party of companions, made his way as far north as Stornoway to seek a ship to take him to France. There he was unsuccessful and retraced his steps to meet up with Flora MacDonald in South Uist. Though her family were not Jacobites, Flora agreed to help the Prince who, dressed as Flora's maid 'Betty Burke', obtained a boat and crew to row them across the Minch to Skye – and freedom.

15. Loch Skipport lies on the eastern seaboard of South Uist and is a narrow arm of the sea which has all the appearance of a canal. The pier was erected in 1879 by the owner of South Uist, Lady Gordon Cathcart, at a cost of nearly £2,000, one of the very few acts of charity this family offered the island. As a mid-way point between Lochboisdale and Lochmaddy, in North Uist, Loch Skipport was more than useful in enabling goods and supplies to be landed. Before the Second World War the main activity on the pier was the shipping of sheep for markets on the Scottish mainland. The ship seen at the pier in the S.S. 'Dunara Castle' owned by the shipping line McCallum Orme. Starting her 6-day trip from the River Clyde, she would steam to the Hebrides, calling in at Castlebay, Lochboisdale, Loch Skipport and Lochmaddy, before visiting the ports on the west coast of Skye. Built in 1875 at Port Glasgow, the 'Dunara Castle' sailed for nearly 75 years in Hebridean waters. She took part in the evacuation of St. Kilda in 1930. She was broken up in 1948.

16. Before there were causeways connecting North Uist and South Uist to Benbecula, the only means of crossing from one island to the other was by foot or horse and cart at low tides. Benbecula ceased to be a separate island in 1943 when the South Bridge was opened after a long campaign by Father O'Regan, parish priest on Benbecula. The bridge is still known locally as 'O' Regan's Bridge'. The North Ford, between Benbecula and North Uist, was opened in 1960 by Her Majesty the Queen Mother. Crossing the fords was always dangerous and required the advice of an expert guide. The departing traveller always left with a prayer: 'Faothail mhath dhuibh' — A good ford to you. The guides were often hard put to it to trace safe new tracks after each winter's storms had brought changes. Quicksands had to be avoided. The ford was open for about one hour on either side of low water and the route was marked by beacons and cairns or 'weed-covered stones which show well against the white sand'. This picture, c. 1910, shows two carts making their way carefully across the sand. Ben Eaval is seen in the background.

17. The island group of St. Kilda lies in the deep Atlantic about 40 miles west of the island of Lewis. St. Kilda was evacuated in 1930 and is now occupied by an army rocket-tracking station. Each year working parties of visitors land on the main island, Hirta, to restore the old houses and to keep the other buildings in reasonable repair. In 1986 St. Kilda was designated as Scotland's first World Heritage Site by UNESCO, joining such famous places as the pyramids in Egypt and the Taj Mahal. This picture. taken c. 1890, shows part of 'Main Street' with its typical stone-built Hebridean houses and some of the islanders. They are, however, not descended from the original St. Kildans. During its recorded history St. Kilda virtually lost its whole population twice and had to be re-populated from people from the Hebrides. The highest population (180) recorded was in 1697. Thirty-six people deserted the island in 1930. The main reason for the violent fluctuation in the population was disease, usually brought in by visitors, such as the 'boat cold', and epidemics of smallpox and cholera. The staple diet was potatoes, fish and seabirds.

18. Native St. Kildans pose for the photographer, c. 1890, in the main and only street. Though the islanders seem relaxed here, their lives were a constant battle for survival. Their houses contained only the minimum for basic creature comfort. Driftwood was precious and was fashioned into crude seats and other utensils. They made their own clothes from the wool of the unique Soay sheep, which was plucked rather than sheared. Shoes were made from cow-hide, often simply folded and held together with a leather thong. For light they used the 'cruisgean', a simple lamp containing bird oil with a piece of cloth as the wick. Everything on the island existed for the common good. Gifts brought in by visitors were divided up between the families. Island produce, such as tweed cloth, feathers, cheese, wool, salted fish and fulmar oil, was used to pay the rent for the owner of St. Kilda: the Chief of MacLeod at Dunvegan in Skye. The St. Kildans relied greatly on the sea birds for their food. Gannets, fulmars and puffins were caught in large quantities, gutted and dried and stored to last the winter months. Fishing was also carried out when the weather permitted.

19. This picture, c. 1920, shows the 'St. Kilda Parliament', whose members governed the life of the community. There was no leader with all decisions taken on unanimous agreement. Once the assembly was convened, the Parliament would consider the type of work to be done: bird-catching, fishing or visiting the neighbouring islands. They looked after the distribution of birds caught, and ensured that old and sick people received a share of the catch. In the opening years of this century the islanders faced recurrent epidemics, a scourge of infantile tetanus and successive failures of the harvest. They began to discuss the possibility of total evacuation, which had first been proposed in 1875 with a plan to take the entire population to Canada. In 1928 the population had fallen to 37 and in the following year an epidemic of wet eczema broke out. It was the last straw. On 10 May 1930 the last of the St. Kildans bade farewell to their island home to be settled on the Scottish mainland. The only St. Kildans now remaining are the wren, the mouse and the Soay sheep, all unique sub-species.

20. Lochmaddy is the 'capital' of North Uist and has a current population of around 400. The scattered nature of its houses and public buildings tends to detract from its official status. The township derives its name from three curiously shaped rocks in the entrance to the harbour, called 'maddies', derived from the Gaelic word for a dog. In the 17th century Lochmaddy was an important fishing and curing station but then went into a decline which lasted until the herring boom years in the middle of last century. Becoming the public centre for North Uist, it saw the building of a cottage hospital, hotel, bank, court house, prison and post office. The buildings shown here are the imposing County Buildings which housed the officials who administered the island. A poorhouse was built late last century, with a rather generous capacity for inmates which was never realised. The Report of the Poor Law Commission, 1909, stated: 'The Lochmaddy Poorhouse was a gross and stupid blunder, carried out by influences ignorant of the requirement of these districts, and really in direct opposition to public opinion. It is of absolutely no value.'

21. As Lochmaddy slowly became a port of call for the steamships plying the waters of the Minch, it was natural to have a hotel built close to the pier. The picture (c. 1900) shows the Lochmaddy Hotel (1863) thirty years after it was constructed. The hotel was built on the site of an 18th century inn. The pier at Lochmaddy was built during the Uist ownership of Sir John Powlett Orde. Originally it consisted of a concrete embankment with a wooden structure of greenheart piles covered by a wooden decking. Its construction allowed the berthing of ships and the easier off-loading of goods and passengers who, no doubt, viewed the comforts of the hotel with some anticipation. Its clientele included officials of Inverness-shire County Council, which had all the southern isles under its jurisdiction, lawyers attending cases in the Court House, commercial travellers touting their various wares and fishermen and sportsmen. The latter were attracted to the wildlife of North Uist which had been newly opened up to the rod and the gun. The crofters, however, regarded the sportsmen as nuisances because they disturbed livestock and trampled over growing crops. Often encounters ended up in fights, and sore heads.

22. The township of Sollas in North Uist, c. 1930. As can be seen the houses have been greatly improved from the old days of the black houses. In 1849 this crofting township was under orders for the eviction of its population by Lord MacDonald of Sleat in Skye, who owned North Uist. The people naturally resisted and in July a ship, the 'Cygnet', sailed from Skye with 33 policemen and various officials to carry out the eviction. Landing at Lochmaddy, the force marched to Sollas where two crofters were arrested as the ringleaders. A day of talking followed with no result. The policemen then began to enter each house and throw out both occupants and domestic property. The thatched roofs were ripped off and the timbers made ready for firing. A bloody battle then ensued. A local minister eventually managed to pacify both sides and only a token eviction was carried out. This picture was taken only a couple of decades after the large farm at Sollas was broken up to form crofts, with the new settlers being given loans for houses. Near Sollas is a site on which excavations have revealed continuous human habitation going back to Neolithic times.

23. The crofting township of Hougharry, North Uist, c. 1900. Situated on the Atlantic-facing seaboard of the island, the compact nature of the old 'baile' or township can be seen here. It takes the traditional form of a nucleated settlement. Hougharry was never cleared of its people and has thus remained reasonably intact. New houses continued to be built on the sites of their predecessors. The local pattern of land use has changed little over the years. Close by Hougharry is an old churchyard which surrounds the site of an ancient chapel dedicated to St. Mary. Virtually all traces of it have long been obliterated, but the largest tomb of Clan Ranald (dated 1768) is thought to have occupied the site. Broken stone crosses from all ages are scattered about the overgrown churchyard.

24. This picture, c. 1920, shows a typical Uist market day. The main function of the market was to buy and sell livestock, including horses, sheep and cattle. Buyers from the Scottish mainland were always eager to get the good quality cattle for which Uist had a reputation. The market day was also something of a social occasion when the people from remote townships took the opportunity to meet with friends and relatives and to catch up with the news of the day. Women took advantage of the many stalls which offered such articles as hats, ribbons, handkerchiefs and, perhaps, a piece of silk as a special personal luxury. A description of an island market day, dated around 1890, says: 'Sellers and buyers have done their business, and all have now abandoned themselves to merriment... On a smooth bit of green a ragged bagpiper and a blind fiddler are playing different tunes, and shepherds, herd-girls, farm-women and drovers are dancing like mad people, with the usual shrieks that accompany the Highland reel. Naturally there was a liberal consumption of the 'barley bree' at the market but, the consumers being all hardened vessels, no-one appeared any the worse.'

25. North Uist has many witnesses to the ancient past. This picture, c. 1900, shows a monolith and the remains of a dun. The stone is Clach Mor an Che, 'The Big Stone of the World', and stands 2.5m high. Nearby can be seen the remains of Dun na Carnaich (Fort of the Cairn). The island tradition has it that wrongdoers were tied to the stone. One historian has suggested that the Stone's name derives from Che, who was one of the seven sons of Cruithne, an eponymous ancestor of the Picts, the race which occupied Scotland before the Gaels came across from Ireland. The Dun is a chambered cairn which once consisted of an inner chamber over which a great pile of stones was placed. A passage was left to allow access to the chamber for the remains of the dead to be deposited. The existence of these chambered cairns gives rise to speculation that the Hebrides were once populated some 4,000 years ago with a society which was well-organised and had its 'religious' beliefs ordered sufficiently to consider the use of massive stone monuments to commemorate events and special occasions, such as the death of a chief.

26. Among the hills of North Uist is the highest concentration of chambered cairns in all the Hebrides. The stone circle shown here is situated close by Barpa Langass, a massive chambered cairn 24m in diameter. An excavation carried out in 1911 revealed Neolithic pottery, flint objects, Bronze Age Beaker pottery and a cremated human bone. The cairn is in a remarkable state of preservation and the inner chamber can still be entered. The stone circle, shown here being visited by a curious visitor, is known as Pobull Fhinn, the People of Fionn, a hero in Celtic mythololgy. It is irregularly oval in shape and sits on a platform which seems to have been partly man-made. There are 24 stones, including large boulders, but it is not certain how many of the latter belong to the circle. Pobull Fhinn is the finest of its kind in North Uist. Ancient tradition has it that the stones represent people who were petrified for misdeeds. The building to the right of the picture is Langass Lodge, built to accommodate shooting parties, guests of the owner of North Uist. It is now a hotel.

27. Tarbert, Isle of Harris, c. 1900. Lying in the crook of East Loch Tarbert, the village consists of about two dozen houses perched on the rocky hillside. The name 'Tarbert' is derived from the fact that about a half mile to the west lies West Loch Tarbert, with the conjoining isthmus barely preventing Harris from being divided into two parts. As the main port of call for Harris, the village was well-provided for with shops, a number specialising in the sale of Harris Tweed which, at the turn of the century, was a popular cloth and largely woven in Harris, before the industry was to be concentrated in Stornoway, Lewis. At the time, the cloth was completely hand-made, from washing the wool, carding, spinning, dyeing and weaving. Tarbert received some kind of official status when it was given a sub-post office in 1836. Even so, it took a full fortnight for a letter posted at Tarbert to reach Fort William in Inverness-shire, because it was carried most of the way by runner. Full status was given to Tarbert when the telegraph arrived in 1872. From then on Tarbert became the 'capital' of Harris.

28. The pier at Tarbert, c. 1905. In common with all Hebridean ports of call, the locals congregate, out of curiosity, to see who comes off the steamer. The ship just arriving at the pier is the S.S. 'Hebrides'. Built at Troon in 1898 for McCallum's West Highland trade she was a familiar sight in the main ports in the islands. Along with the 'Dunara Castle', she was a popular cruising vessel, often employed on extended summer trips to St. Kilda. Her latter years were spent carrying cargo and livestock. She was broken up in 1955, after nearly sixty years of service plying the waters of the islands. The turn of the century saw an ever-increasing demand by tourists for sailing holidays to provide something to talk about when they got back home. Like many of her kind the 'Hebrides' was a comparatively small ship, of 585 tons gross. But they plied the island routes all year round through weather fair and foul 'steadily plodding their path from port to port, entering silent little lochs to discharge a cargo, or anchoring off some little townships to take on board sheep or cattle if it be at the time of the sales'.

29. Discharging cargo and passengers at the Tarbert pier. For the two or three hours during which the ship was berthed, Tarbert was the scene of much activity. Postmen collected mail bags. Shopkeepers waited anxiously for the supplies they needed to restock their shelves with the luxuries which the city folk took for granted. And the inevitable sportsmen and anglers waited impatiently for their cases and trunks to be off-loaded, eager to be off to try their hand at deer-stalking and fishing for salmon on the hills and rivers of Harris. A few hours later the pier would be deserted with Tarbert settling back into its easy-going pace once more − until the next arrival of the S.S. 'Hebrides'.

HARRIS HOTEL AND EAST LOCH. TARBERT.

30. The Harris Hotel, c. 1920. It was originally built in 1865 as a Lodge by the Earls of Dunmore who had purchased Harris from Lt. Col MacLeod in 1834 (including St. Kilda) for £60,000. The main function of the lodge was to accommodate guests for an overnight stay, before they travelled to the Earl's Harris home, Amhuinnsuidhe Castle (see No. 33) for fishing and deer-stalking holidays. Some of the imported stone which was used to build the Castle went into the Harris Hotel. Some of the hotel guests can be seen standing on the front steps, while the chauffered car waits their pleasure. This car is one of the Fords from Lews Castle, Stornoway. For many years the Harris Hotel was only one of two such establishments in Harris and was something of a Mecca for tourists while they explored the hinterland. The motor car, used by the hotel guests, often took passengers the 40 miles to Stornoway, there being at the time this picture was taken only one bus service a week between Stornoway and Tarbert.

31. This picture, c. 1905, shows an unusual Hebridean industry: whaling. The station was set up at Bunamhuinneadar, near Tarbert, just before the turn of the century by a Norwegian whaling company. The equipment was brought from Ireland and re-erected on the north shore of West Loch Tarbert. It operated until the outbreak of the First World War and re-commenced operations in 1918. In 1922 Lord Leverhulme, who owned Lewis for a few years, bought the operation on behalf of Lever Bros, partly to provide employment but also because he suspected that the Norwegians were deliberately contaminating the Hebridean herring grounds with whale offal to drive the herring to Norway. The station was repaired and in 1923 three vessels were purchased to catch whales in the North Atlantic. But the venture was a financial failure. The Norwegians had been converting the whale carcasses into guano. Leverhulme's idea was to produce oil and turn the meat into sausages for African natives. The oil was to be used with the whale meat 'to improve the possibilities of mastication, as whale meat is rather tough'. He also came up with the idea of producing smoked whalemeat for exporting to the Congo.

32. St. Clement's Church, at Rodel, South Harris, is one of the most outstanding structures of its kind in the West of Scotland. It is also the only considerable architectural monument in the Hebrides. The church was built c. 1500 on the site of an earlier structure. It is constructed of rubble, dressed with schist and imported freestone. The external walls are covered with carvings and sculptured panels: the tower is some 20m high. In the first half of the 16th century it was extensively repaired by Alexander MacLeod of Harris, who died in 1547 and whose remarkable tomb it houses. MacLeod prepared his tomb nineteen years before he died and he must have been proud of it, for it is reckoned to be the finest of its kind in Scotland. It is elaborately wrought, with nine sculptured panels covering the rear wall of the tomb's alcove, and the recumbent effigy of an armed warrior. Also buried here is Mary MacLeod, a Gaelic poet of the 17th century who was governess to the young MacLeods of Dunvegan. On her death she expressed a wish to be buried at Rodel, face down to be in everlasting contact with her native soil.

Amhuinnsuidhe Castle, Harris

33. This picture, c. 1890, shows Amhuinnsuidhe Castle in the west of Harris. Originally called Fincastle, it was built c. 1866 by Lord Dunmore who purchased Harris in 1834 for £60,000. Lady Dunmore started off the now famous Harris Tweed industry, though in her day it was a simple cottage-based activity. She became interested in the quality of work produced by two Harris sisters and thought that the cloth could be marketed to bring much-needed income to the people of Harris. Harris Tweed made an impact in London where its hard-wearing qualities were ideal for outdoor clothing. Within a few years demand outstripped production and an organised industry was born. The castle has had a number of owners since Lord Dunmore sold North Harris to Sir Edward Scott in 1868 and is now owned by a Swiss financier. It was in Amhuinnsuidhe Castle, during a holiday as the guest of Sir E. Scott, that J.M. Barrie conceived the idea for a play which is undeniably Hebridean: 'Mary Rose.' In the play, the 'Isle that likes to be visited' is situated in the locality of the castle, but has yet to be identified.

34. Crofters' houses just outside Stornoway, Lewis, c. 1905. This was a typical scene throughout Lewis of the time. The only substantial stone-built houses in Lewis were farm-houses, church manses, hunting lodges and, of course, most of the buildings in the town of Stornoway. At the turn of the century the crofters supported their families with what they grew on their few acres of land, milk, butter and cheese from a cow and some wages earned from the herring fishing. Notice the attempt to brighten up the houses with whitewash. The house in the foreground has its thatch held down by ropes tied to stones, while the house behind uses a rope net for security. Behind the man standing at the doorway is a small byre in which the cow was sheltered overnight and during the winter months. To the right of the picture is a large peat stack. The cutting of peat for fuel was an essential 'right' because few of the Lewis people could afford the expense of coal. And, in a treeless island, there was no wood, except that which might have been washed ashore during storms at sea. The children seem reasonably happy with their lot.

Crofter's Cottage, Lewis (Woman Knitting)

*This is not like they all are.*

35. A crofter's cottage in a more remote part of Lewis, c. 1900. Note the rough stones used in its construction with large boulders forming the foundation of the outer wall. Between the outer and inner walls, some 2m apart, earth and rubble was packed in to make the building more substantial. Despite their appearance, the houses were built with an expertise often drawn from the need to set up new dwellings when the Lewis people were 'cleared' from one place to settle in another part of the island. The women is dressed in typical home-woven cloth. She is knitting a woollen stocking, either for the family or else for sale in Stornoway to earn some pin money. The creel on her back was used to carry anything from peats to taking fish into Stornoway. If her husband was away at the herring fishing, she would have to do all the croft work and look after the family. The interior of the house was simply furnished with the floor made of hard-packed earth kept dry by the heat of the fire. Formerly the fire was in the centre of the house, but later was shifted to one gable end.

Taking Home Peats, Stornoway

*This is coals they burn here*

36. The ubiquitous creels used for carrying home dried peat for the fire, c. 1900. As in the previous picture, the women's hands are seldom idle. Here the young women are knitting stockings which they could sell to earn a shilling or two to buy some small personal belonging. In the summer months in Lewis, many women took the cattle to the moor for grazing. This was known as going to the 'sheilings', a form of transhumance which was common throughout Europe. While living in rough huts called 'airidh', the women would make butter and cheese in sufficient quantities to help the household through the winter months. During the decades when the herring fishing industry was at its height, many young Lewis women went to work as herring gutters and followed the fishing as it moved from Yarmouth, Lowestoft, Eyemouth, Fraserburgh, Buckie, Wick and Shetland. Once the herring shoals turned into the Minch waters, Stornoway took on the proportions of a boom town, and the local herring girls were recruited in large numbers.

37. This old building is the most important religious edifice to have been dedicated to St. Columba, who found the Celtic Church on the island of Iona in 563 AD. There is no record of whether Columba travelled in the Hebrides. However, from Iona many missionaries made the journey to remote parts of the west Highlands and Islands. No doubt St. Catan, the monk who landed here just outside Stornoway, decided that Columba's name should be honoured rather than his own. Just as Iona is the last resting place for many of Scotland's kings, St. Columba's church is the burial place of nineteen Chiefs of the Clan MacLeod who were dominant in Lewis until c. 1600. The earliest record of the building dates from 1506. Inside the building are two elaborately carved slabs, one bearing the effigy of Roderick VII of Lewis and dates from the end of the 15th century. Another slab of ornate design commemorates Margaret, the daughter of Roderick, who was the mother of John, the last Abbot of Iona. So the Iona connection stretches back a millennium. The 5th Earl of Seaforth, who took over Lewis from the MacLeods, also lies here.

38. The Standing Stones at Callanish, Lewis, which are rated second only to Stonehenge in the south of England. They were erected c. 2000 BC and have remained upright to the present day. When Lewis was purchased by Sir James Matheson, his attention was drawn to the stones which were then deep in the peat which had grown up around them. He authorized the removal of the peat in 1857 to reveal the stones. This picture, c. 1900, shows the bleached appearance of the lower part of the stones in sharp contrast to the upper parts which are dark with lichen growth. In plan, the layout of the stones looks like a Celtic Cross, which gave the suggestion that the stones had a Christian significance. Over the centuries many traditions have grown up about the stones, though modern theorists suggest they were a lunar calendar. One story associates the stone circle with the ceremony held on the first day of May (Beltane) when all fires in the vicinity were extinguished. A new fire was lit by an old priest and the head of each household came to receive a peat ember to rekindle his own fire.

39. This picture of the massive stone tower of Dun Carloway was taken c. 1900. It is located on the west side of Lewis. The duns, also called 'brochs', were built throughout the west and north of Scotland in the period 100 BC to 300 AD. Few of these structures remain today. Their function is still subject to argument. One theory is that they were defensive structures, to be occupied when the local village was under siege. All the inhabitants fled to the safety of the broch. But where would drinking water come from? Wells are generally absent from the broch sites. The Carloway broch walls at their highest remaining part stand some 10m high and are built using the drystone technique, with no mortar, and are very strong due to their double wall construction. The inner wall stands vertically while the outer wall slopes inwards. Within the walls are chambers connected to narrower galleries at higher levels. As late as the 1870s, a Lewis family used the broch as a home: '... a respectable looking family living in the ground flat of the broch'. The 'black house' in the foreground demonstrates the continuity of building construction in Lewis over two millennia.

40. This picture shows Garynahine Lodge, c. 1920. It was one of a number of such buildings erected during the ownership of Lewis by Sir James Matheson last century to accommodate guests at Lews Castle, Stornoway, while they took advantage of fishing in the excellent salmon rivers or stalked deer in the surrounding hills and moors. Occasionally the lodges were let to sportsmen who fished and shot to their hearts content. On the original site of Garynahine Lodge was a building dating from 1720 called the 'Callanish Inn', which one guest described in the 1860s as 'the dirtiest little den it was ever my misfortune to locate in'. The Lodge is now part of the Garynahine Estate which offers salmon fishing to wealthy guests.

41. The Butt of Lewis Lighthouse, c. 1930. This light was one of a number provided by the Northern Lighthouse Board to provide safe navigation for ships coming in from the North Atlantic and the western approaches to the Hebrides. It was built in 1862 to designs by the Stevensons of Edinburgh, a family with a long history of assocation with Scotland's lighthouses. In 1907 a wireless telegraph station was installed to give news of shipping movements past the Butt of Lewis. In November 1940 the lighthouse was machine-gunned by a German plane during the Second World War, but little damage was sustained. The Lighthouse today monitors, by remote control, the lighthouse on the Flannan Isles, about 20 miles out in the Atlantic, which is now an automatic light.

Lewis Castle, Stornoway

42. This imposing pile is Lews Castle, Stornoway, in a picture taken c. 1900. In 1844 Sir James Matheson bought the island of Lewis from the last of the descendants of the Earls of Seaforth who had themselves taken Lewis from the MacLeods around 1600. Sir James made his fortune in the Far East, through his company, Jardine Matheson. A good part of Sir James' money came from the thriving opium trade, which earned him the title 'Sir Drug' from Disraeli in Parliament. Work on the castle started in 1847 and the cost, including the layout of the castle grounds and policies, was over £100,000. Because of the thick layers of peat, earth was imported from the Scottish mainland to enable the newly planted trees to take root. Many exotic species of trees were included in the planting programme. Large glass-covered conservatories were also built to house rare species of plants, no doubt obtained through Sir James' connections with the Far East. The stone for the castle came from a quarry at Dalbeg on the west side of Lewis. In recent years the castle housed a technical college, then a school and is now scheduled to become a Heritage Centre.

43. This is the imposing entrance to the grounds of Lews Castle, c. 1900. Called locally 'Porter's Lodge' its style reflects the mock-Tudor design of the castle. Until about twenty years ago it housed a family but before that it was the dwelling of the gatekeeper whose job it was to vet visitors to the castle. Through these gates have passed many famous personalities, such as King Edward and Queen Alexandra, Sir Harry Lauder, the Scottish comedian and, not least, those high in Stornoway's social order invited to the famous castle balls. In 1918 the island of Lewis was bought by Lord Leverhulme, who founded his soap empire at Port Sunlight, England. He tried to re-vitalise the island's resources and laid plans for the renewal of Stornoway. But problems from ex-servicemen returning from the First World War, who demanded crofts, led to Leverhulme to sell Lewis off piecemeal. His offer of the castle and its policies as a gift in perpetuity to the people of Stornoway was accepted in 1923 and the estate is now run by the Stornoway Trust.

44. This picture, c. 1910, shows the rich furnishings of the drawing room in Lews Castle. As a man with vast wealth at his disposal, Sir James Matheson saw to it that his Lewis home was fitted out for luxurious confort. The furniture and hangings are all mid-Victorian. This room was situated next to the great hall of ballroom, through the double door on the left. It was to the drawing room that privileged guests were invited to rest from the evening's dancing, perhaps to sit and talk of local matters with Sir James (created a Baronet in 1851 'in recognition of his great exertions and munificence in providing the inhabitants of Lewis with food during the severe famine of 1845-46 and succeeding years'). Sir James died in 1878 when his son Donald Matheson, and later his son Duncan Matheson, took over the reforms which Sir James had carried out during his lifetime. Colonel Matheson was to sell Lewis in 1918 to Lord Leverhulme. One wonders whether, in a few quiet moments, Sir James ever reflected on his boyhood in Sutherland, before entering on a business career in London, Calcutta and then in China where his fortune was made.

45. The library of Lews Castle c. 1910. The number of books in this room was not large because the room was, to a large extent, used by gentlemen guests at the castle as a smoking room. It was also used for small and intimate gatherings to listen to music. One popular guest musician was Marjory Kennedy Fraser, who spent many years collecting Hebridean folksongs, now contained in three volumes 'Songs of the Hebrides'. She, with her daughter Patuffa, gave recitals here with Gaelic songs accompanied on the clarsach, a small Highland harp. Sir Harry Lauder the Scots comedian, entertained guests in the library. In 1922 the 'veteran of variety' Charles Cobrun visited the castle and no doubt gave a rendering of the song which made him famous: 'The man who broke the bank at Monte Carlo.' Among other guests who appeared in the castle were Olga Nethersole, a well-known actress in her day, and Raffles Davidson, a popular artist.

46. The dining room of Lews Castle in this picture looks more like a baronial hall, with its massive oak beams. The tapestries on the wall are from the Gobelin factory. The lighting for this room was by gas. A number of lighting fittings in the main rooms were very fine crystal chandeliers which must have added an extra glitter to social occasions. The portrait on the wall to the right of the picture is that of Sir James Matheson. In Lord Leverhulme's time, guests to dinner were piped into the dining room with the piper remaining in the room during the meal, playing at intervals. It is recorded: 'This however, precluded all conversation when he was playing... so he was persuaded to stand in the doorway with the drones of his pipes facing the long hallway to the front door.' On the occasions when Matheson stayed at the castle, he would have had dinner with his estate factor, Donald Munro, known as the 'Chamberlain of Lewis'. He took over the running of Lewis in 1854 and ruled with a rod of iron until his downfall in 1874 as the result of his arrogant and inhuman treatment of crofters.

47. This magnificent structure in white marble is the memorial erected to the memory of Lady Mary Jane Matheson, wife of Sir James. Her maiden name was Perceval, a name which is still used in Stornoway for a road and for Perceval Square. After Sir James died in 1878 the Lewis estate was left for her to administer until her death in 1896. The 1880s of last century were the years during which the crofting population were agitating for crofting rights. Thus, Lady Matheson was faced with many problems to which there were no easy solutions. Those people without homes built them on the common pasture, almost overnight, and were just as quickly demolished by the Estate officers. These actions did much to build up a great feeling of resentment against the Mathesons. Even after the passing of the Crofting Act in 1886, Lady Matheson received regular requests for the break-up of farms into small croft holdings. All were refused on the advice of her estate officials. Though her name is hardly remembered now, the people of Stornoway have to thank her for the part she played in planting the woods surrounding Lews Castle which now belong to the community.

48. Cromwell Street, c. 1910, the main thoroughfare of Stornoway. The building on the extreme left, now a supermarket, was a shop owned by James MacLeod. He sold flour, salt, butter, tea and tobacco. Next to the shop is the British Linen Bank building (1889) now owned by the Bank of Scotland. Built of pink sandstone it is a prominent feature. In the far centre is the old Town House which also acted as a Court House. The street was once known as 'Deemster Street' (deemster — a judge) before the name changed to 'Cromwell'. There are no records to indicate when the name was changed. The army of Oliver Cromwell did occupy Stornoway in the mid-17th century though few traces of their stay remains. It is rather strange, therefore, that a main street in Stornoway should take the name of an English dictator. The building on the right is still known as 'Granite House', from the stone used in its construction. Some indication of the degree of prosperity which the fishing industry brought to the town can be seen in the jewellers shop on the extreme right. The clock tower of the newly built Town Hall adds dignity to the skyline.

*James Street, Stornoway*

49. By the 1880s, the herring industry brought both wealth and employment to the island of Lewis. Stornoway, being a major herring port, benefited from all this activity to the extent that some of the prosperity began to show in the construction of handsome stone-built houses. This picture shows James Street, c. 1910, about a decade or two after the houses were built. The last house in the street bears the date 1886. Most of the streets and roads in Stornoway were not yet properly metalled and in the rainy season the heavy horse-drawn carts created deep ruts wich required the constant attention of the road-menders. On the left of the picture is a small plantation of hawthorn trees which, over the years, leaned to one side, the effects of the south-westerly winds which swept over the island in the winter months. The tall clock tower in the distance is the first building of the Nicolson Institute, a school which, provided through the generosity of a Lewis family, gave the island a much-needed centre for education.

*Stornoway. Bayhead Street.*

50. This is Bayhead Street, c. 1907. Taking advantage of the many people who came in from the country districts in Lewis, where it was difficult to obtain many luxuries, a number of Stornoway worthies developed one room in their houses to create a shop. Bayhead Street was no exception and here we see some of the enterprises, such as the building on the right owned by Angus Morrison. He was a joiner to trade but also offered undertaking services. The building is now a three-storey house with a painter's business on the ground floor. Farther along the street (the white building) was a butcher's shop where one could obtain a Lewis delicacy: a sheep's head, excellent for making broth. On the site now stands the Gospel Hall. At the time this picture was taken there were two or three houses with thatched roofs, in one of which was yet another shop selling groceries. One well-known shop was owned by 'Kenny Captain', who made his name during the First World War by selling 'near beer'. This was a wartime brew known as 'Lloyd George Beer' or 'Munition Ale', a liquid concoction which looked like cold tea and had a slightly acidic taste.

51. This scene is the upper end of Point Street, looking to Francis Street, c. 1906. The truncated tower on the right is the uncompleted part of Martin's Memorial Church (1878) which had to wait 25 years before it was given its steeple and spire. The building on the right is the Town Hall recently opened to accommodate the Public Library and the offices of Stornoway Town Council. The shop on the left is the 'emporium' of MacPherson & Co., the chief chemist of which was Roderick Smith, later to become a Provost of the Council. Mr. Smith later took over the business and moved to the building (centre left) at the corner of Point Street, where it is today. The shop just up from the Town Hall on the right was the Drapery and General Store owned by Matthew Russell. There is a well-known story about Russell when a trade war broke out between him and another shopkeeper in the town. To fend off the competition, Russell advertised: 'See for yourselves. Russell's Trousers are Down. Inspection Invited.' When the opposition reduced his trouser prices even lower, Russell responded by another advertisement: 'Russell's Trousers Down Again!'

52. The newly formed Lewis Pipe Band brings out a crowd of interested spectators in North Beach Street, c. 1910. The band was established in 1904 and over eighty years later the band still gives public performances during the summer months. Perceval Square, on the right, is named after Lady Mary Jane Matheson wife of Sir James Matheson. The tall building in the distance is the 'Sail Loft' used for the storage of herring nets. It is not recorded when it was built but it is reckoned to date to c. 1790. It now houses the offices and stores of the Stornoway Fishermen's Co-operative, thus retaining its long-standing link with the fishing industry. The three-storey building (left), covered with white stucco, is the Lewis Hotel bearing the date of its completion: 1829. It is thus one of the few very old buildings in Stornoway. It is still run as an hotel. In the centre left are the offices of the National Bank of Scotland now occupied by the Royal Bank of Scotland. On the middle right are the ruins of the old church of St. Lennan, once the parish church in the 17th century and now vanished to become a car park.

53. Part of South Beach Street, c. 1910. On the left can be seen what was once a common sight on Stornoway's piers up until the 1930s: mountains of barrels which were filled with salted herring. The building on the right is the Imperial Hotel, later to become a girls' hostel, accommodating pupils from the hinterland of Lewis who had to stay in town during the school sessions. The building to the right of the Town Hall is where Matthew Russell moved his business. The upper storeys of the building is the Waverley Hotel, so called because it features carved heads of characters from Sir Walter Scott's novels. This picture was obviously taken when the herring fleet was out at sea. The herring girls seem to be taking advantage of a respite in their work, which often started early in the morning and could carry on until midnight, gutting herring and packing them into barrels. This had to be done because the herring has a soft flesh which could not be left to decay. The man in the centre of the street carries a box of Tate & Lyle sugar cubes and what looks suspiciously like a 'pig' of whisky.

54. The lower end of South Beach Street, c. 1910. To the right is the south beach, a small strand of sand which has never been developed since the 'Fife Adventurers' landed in Lewis in 1598. These were colonists spurred on by rather exaggerated accounts of the wealth of the island. Their venture was to be disastrous for they failed to recognise that the wealth of the Hebrides lay in the seas around the island. In this picture fishing boats are drawn up for repair and maintenance. In the left corner a fisherman is filling tanks from the water hydrant. The building on the left is the old Caledonian Hotel, which was destroyed by fire about twenty years ago and has since been replaced by a more modern structure. The house on the right, just before the Town Hall, was Carn House. In this house was born in 1754 Colin MacKenzie who was to become Surveyor-General of all India. MacKenzie took a great interest in the country of his adoption and amassed a huge collection of antiques. Some of the collection is now in the Victoria & Albert Museum, London, with the remainder still in Madras.

55. South Beach, c. 1925. The motor car has now been introduced to Lewis, though it caught on slowly with the horse-drawn vehicle being the dominant and preferred mode of transport. The water hydrant now seems rather neglected. One can just make out, over the roof of the car on the right, one of the gas-lit lampposts which were to give Stornoway's streets their public lighting. The building on the right, just past the white stuccoed house, is the Star Inn. In 1803, James Hogg, the Border poet, paid a visit to Stornoway and stayed in a lodging house on the Star Inn site. On not a few occasions he was disturbed by fights between the town's Collector of Taxes and a bailiff: 'It was fought with great spirit and monstrous vociferation. Desperate wounds were given and received, the door was split in pieces and twice some of the party entered my chamber.' Hogg found that the town had no brewery, no bakery, no barber but had 'elegant houses and genteel inhabitants'. The lorry on the left is built from a basic Model T Ford chassis.

56. This is Kenneth Street, c. 1915. The houses reflect the increase in standards during the previous century when most of the dwellings were small rough-built thatched cottages. During the latter years of last century Kenneth Street was known for the number of 'shebeens' (no fewer than seventeen) which sold strong liquors such as whisky, rum and brandy. These were illicit drink shops frequented by the many men who came to Stornoway with the herring fishing: curers, salesmen, coopers (barrel-makers) and fishermen. Drunkeness was, however, not a great problem, though those who advocated temperance tended to exaggerate the situation. Around the turn of the century most of the licensed premises in Lewis were concentrated in the town. In 1900, for instance, there were only three licensed premises in the islands, all in the town. The shebeens, therefore, catered for those who required what is summed up in a Gaelic proverb: 'Better the little fire that will warm than the great fire that will burn.' The appearance of Kenneth Street has changed only a little over the years and in this picture the thatched shebeens have gone to become respectable dwelling houses.

57. This picture, taken in 1910, shows a good crowd of the folk of Stornoway gathering in Perceval Square to hear the announcement of the accession of King George V to the throne on the death of King Edward VII. The Square, the only open space where public announcements could be made, was named after the wife of Sir James Matheson. To the right of centre can be seen part of the ornate wrought iron fountain which has now disappeared. It was a popular feature when it was working: spraying a huge jet of water upwards, falling into the top basin and then overflowing into a large trough, a favourite with thirsty horses. The building in the background is the old post office, which still stands, but is now the headquarters of the Stornoway Trust, a body set up in 1923 when Lord Leverhulme gifted Lews Castle, its wooded policies and 64,000 acres of Lewis to the people of Stornoway and the island. No doubt some of those listening to the Proclamation might remember the time, in 1902, when King Edward and Queen Alexandra visited Stornoway and stayed at Lews Castle as the guest of Major Duncan Matheson.

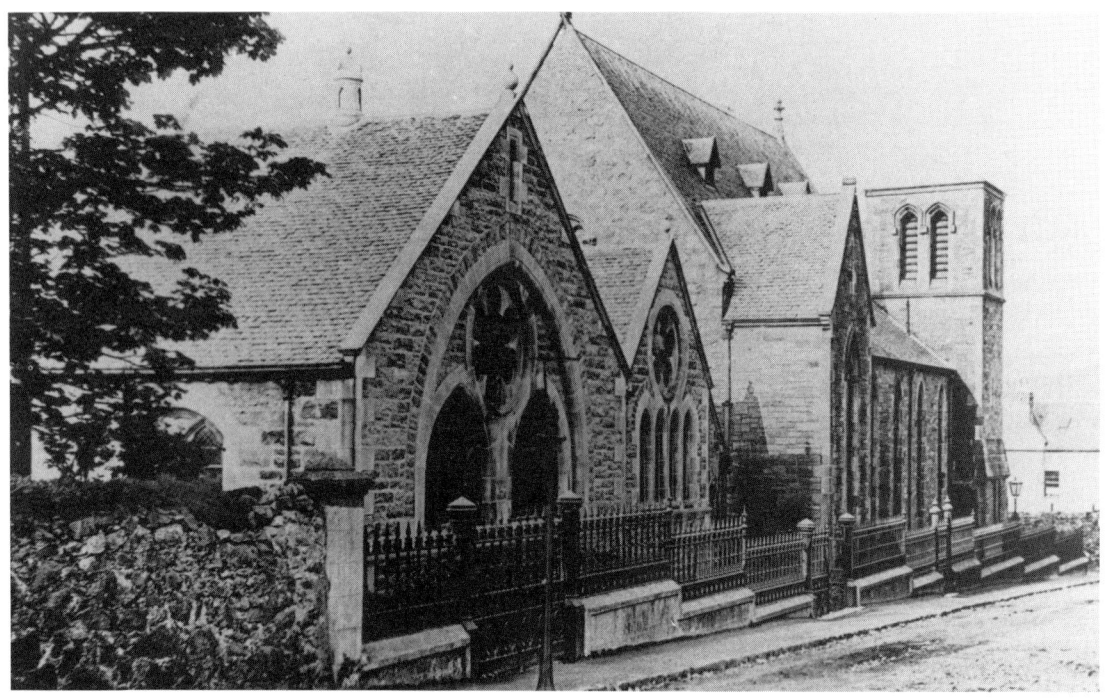

58. This picture is of Martin's Memorial Church on Francis Street, c. 1900. For many years last century all church services were in Gaelic. But as Stornoway became more cosmopolitan those who came for the herring fishing demanded sermons in English. This led to the setting up in 1875 of an English Preaching Mission station and the appointment of Dr. Donald Martin as its first minister (1876). Thereafter work was started on this church which was opened for worship in October 1878. The church hall on the left was completed about 1890. The church spire was not erected until 1911. The church is situated on the corner of Kenneth Street and Francis Street, on the site of the birthplace (1764) of Sir Alexander MacKenzie, who emigrated to Canada with his father around 1774. He went into the fur trade with the North West Company and was soon recognised for his abilities, not least of which was exploring. MacKenzie discovered in 1793 the mouth of the Canadian river which now bears his name. He was knighted for his exploits in both the Arctic and in the Pacific. His book 'Voyages' was in Napoleon's possession during the latter's exile on St. Helena.

PRINCE CHARLIE'S CAIRN, SEAFORTH LOCH. ISLE OF LEWIS. (H.R.H. PRINCE CHARLES EDWARD LANDED, EVENING 4TH MAY 1746.)

59. This cairn was built at the turn of the century at Arnish Point, at the entrance to Stornoway harbour. After the Battle of Culloden in April 1746, Prince Charlie made his way to the Hebrides to escape from the English army but with the price of £30,000 on his head. He and his companions travelled through Harris and Lewis to reach Stornoway on the evening of 4 May 1746. Lewis was then in possession of the Earl of Seaforth but the Earl refused to become involved in the Jacobite cause. This, despite the fact that plans for an aborted Rising were laid in Seaforth Lodge in 1719, near where Lews Castle now stands. While attempts were made to obtain a ship in Stornoway which would take the Prince to France and relative safety, he stayed at the farmhouse owned by Mrs. MacKenzie of Kildun. His presence at Arnish created consternation in the town. Even so, despite the huge reward offered for the Prince's capture, no person in Stornoway offered a ship. Rather the townspeople requested that he leave Lewis quickly! The Prince then made his way south to South Uist where he met Flora MacDonald. The rest is history.

60. This picture of the lighthouse at Arnish Point was taken c. 1890. It was built in 1852 from a design by Alan Stevenson. There was a problem with the sunken reef shown on the right and this led to the invention by Thomas Stevenson of the 'apparent light' which was used to mark pierheads and other sunken rocks. The idea was to erect glass prisms in a beacon which were then illuminated by a beam of light projected from the neighbouring shore. The intention was to produce a light which seemed to come from the beacon itself. The idea was first tried out at Arnish and it was reported that 'the deception is so perfect that the fishermen will not believe that there is not a light there'. This iron beacon, also erected in 1852, took the form of a prefabricated iron tower of plates fixed together and lined with wood. It remained in use for about fifty years and is seen in the picture. The Arnish light became 'unmanned' in 1963 and is now operated automatically.

61. This picture of the Lewis War Memorial dates from c. 1930. Compared with many other memorials to the dead of two world wars, this magnificent structure might seem to be an expression of excess. It is, however, more an expression of the great loss of young men which Lewis suffered. In addition to the men of the regular forces, to which the island made a large contribution, and the Royal Naval Reserve, Lewismen numbering thousands formed practically the whole of the 3rd Special Reserve Battalion of the Seaforth Highlanders, and were in the 3rd Gordons and the 3rd Camerons. Lewis lost 1,151 men out of 6,712 serving, some 17 percent. Practically every fit man in the island was early in the forces. If the ratio of the killed to the total population (29,603) is considered, the island paid twice as much as the rest of the British Isles in sacrifice. The island suffered a further tragedy with the sinking of the 'Iolaire' on New Year's morning, 1919, when over 200 servicemen were drowned just outside Stornoway harbour. The War Memorial was unveiled on 5 September 1924 by Lord Leverhulme, his last public act in Lewis.

62. This picture will bring back memories for those of an older Stornoway generation. It is the fish mart, c. 1920. It was built before the turn of the century to house the many offices of fish salesmen who were eager to bid for the herring catches brought in by sailing wherries and steam drifters. The Fish Mart was octagonal in shape and its hall was used by the fishermen to display their catches. The picture shows baskets of sample fish being brought into the mart for the attention of the buyers. At one time a flagstaff stood in front of the mart to mark the site of the old Stornoway Castle, the stronghold for many generations of Chiefs of the Clan MacLeod. Its ruined walls were visible until the turn of the century when its ancient stones, and the spit of rock on which it stood, disappeared under the new No. 1 pier. A plaque on the present-day Maritime Building commemorates the old castle. The fish mart was demolished about twenty years ago to make way for harbour improvements. The building behind the mart, on the right, is now the watch room of the Stornoway Pier and Harbour Commission.

63. The Stornoway post office in Perceval Square, c. 1905. In 1741 there is a reference to postal bags being made up in Edinburgh for Stornoway but there was no official receiving office. The lack of a postal service created immense difficulties for the commander of the troops who had garrisoned Stornoway since the 1745 Jacobite Rebellion as he had no means of quick communication to the mainland. In 1756 a post office was established at Stornoway with George MacKenzie, steward and receiver of Lewis, appointed as postmaster. Mails were sent across the Minch to Poolewe, where a runner was employed to take the packets to Achnasheen, there to meet a horse-post running to Inverness. By 1833 a branch of the National Bank of Scotland had opened up for business in the town and the hitherto inefficient system of taking mails to the mainland was improved. The earliest recorded postmark dates from the later 1750s but it was not until 1841 that Stornoway received its first datestamp. The post office shown here began its official business in 1855, rented from Sir James Matheson. It also housed the telegraph office. As many as 1,000 telegrams were handled each day.

64. The advent of the parcel post in 1883 meant a great increase in the workload of the Stornoway post office, which, in a 1895 Report, resulted in the postmaster being reprimanded for his unsatisfactory performance. In 1903 the Perceval Square Post Office was condemned as being overcrowded and unhealthy, and a new Crown Office, constructed specifically for the purpose, was proposed. The result was the new post office, on Francis Street, shown here, c. 1910, which was opened in 1908. When the old post office was abandoned in 1906, the mails were handled in temporary premises in the Town Hall. Though much extended at the rear of the building, the post office is still in use, as are the letter-boxes in the wall on the right.

65. The bad housing conditions in Lewis contributed to the occurrence of many ailments and diseases such as dysentry, jaundice and cholera. Tuberculosis was prevalent. In 1795 Lewis had only one doctor. By the turn of this century there were resident medical officers in each parish and five doctors in Stornoway. In 1892 matters came to a head with agitation to build a hospital: 'A well-equipped medical and surgical hospital was an urgent necessity for the island of Lewis.' A committee was appointed to collect funds, the subscription list being headed by the Mathesons of Lews Castle. Funds flowed in from Lewis exiles in many parts of the world. In 1896 the Lewis Cottage Hospital was opened, with fifteen beds. An extension was opened in 1915 when a surgeon and an ambulance were provided. Another extension, in 1929, was paid for by a gift of £3,000 from Mr. John Bain of Chicago, an emigrant son of Lewis who was President of 14 banks in the mid-West. This picture, dating from c. 1910, shows the original hospital building some of the nurses taking a few minutes off their work to pose for the photographer.

66. Stornoway is a Burgh of Barony, with its Charter dating from 18 October 1607. Because of opposition from Scottish mainland towns such as Inverness, Stornoway never achieved Royal Burgh status. In 1862 the town became a Police Burgh under the control of a Chief Magistrate. Under an Act of 1892 the designation 'Town Council' superseded that of 'Burgh Commission' and the Chief Magistrate assumed the title of Provost. In 1897 the suggestion was mooted that some form of Municipal Buildings be provided. Cost was a problem, but this was partially solved when Dr. Andrew Carnegie, who had made a fortune in steel and railways in America, offered to contribute £1,000 towards the construction of a library, provided the town adopted the Public Libraries Act. This was done and the Town Council decided to incorporate the library into a larger structure. The final building is seen in the picture, c. 1910. The cost of construction was £11,000. It was opened in September 1905 by Lord Roseberry. Its life was short-lived. A fire in March 1918 reduced the structure to a shell and it was not until 1929 that the Town Hall was restored and re-opened for business.

*Nicolson Institute, Infant and Elementary Depts., Stornoway*

67. Until the 19th century education in Lewis was a hit or miss affair. Col. Colin MacKenzie, born in Stornoway and highly educated, became Surveyor-General of all India. His sister had to have her letters to him written by another. During last century a number of schools were provided throughout Lewis by various charitable church agencies. In Stornoway the main school was provided by James MacKay, supported by Sir James Matheson. There was also a Female Industrial School on Keith Street, opened in 1848 by Lady Matheson. With the advent of the 1872 Education Act, the Nicolson Institution was set up in MacKay's School in 1873 supported by a bequest from a Stornoway engineer, Alexander Nicolson, who died in Shanghai in 1865. His brothers also decided to donate funds to the new school; they lived as far apart as Yorkshire, Western Australia, South Africa and the Mississippi. In 1888 the Nicolson Institution became the Nicolson Public School, but its name was changed again in 1901 to the Nicolson Institute. The first new school building is shown here, c. 1910, with its impressive clock tower. Today, on its site, is a sports centre, though the tower has been retained.

68. This is the Court House on Lewis Street, c. 1910, built around 1850. The most common crimes in Lewis during the 18th and 19th century were sheep-stealing, assault and illegal distilling. Murder or attempted murder was very rare. Sheep-stealers were punished by being taken 'from the Bar to the Tolbooth of this village' and led through the streets wearing a placard 'SHEEP STEALING'. Sometimes serious wrongdoers were flogged in public. The practice of pillorying took place on market days and Sundays. The first and only murder in Lewis this century occurred in 1969. Old Court Records relating to Lewis go back to c. 1788 and include mentions of ship wrecking. In 1824 two men were fined £4 when Lloyds of London brought a case against them for the destruction of a ship's mast which they had found washed up on the shore. During the time when shebeens were a dominant feature in Kenneth Street, a number of the owners were frequently in Court. One case records that when the Customs men broke into a shebeen they found a number of kegs of spirits, and a notice saying 'Try No. 4. It is sure to Please'.

69. This view, taken from one of the towers of Lews Castle, is of Stornoway's inner harbour and dates from c. 1908. The scarcity of herring ships in the bay indicates that it was taken in the winter months. The deserted street and Perceval Square, with its iron fountain, on the left also suggests that this was a Sunday. On this one day of the week hardly anything stirred. However, Martin's Memorial Church, seen mid-centre right, and the Free Presbyterian Church, just off centre left, would have been packed full with worshippers. The white building to the left is the Royal Hotel which was closed for a number of years to be re-opened for business in 1926 'newly refurnished and decorated'. The large building (centre front) is known locally as 'Gladstone House', after the British Prime Minister W.E. Gladstone, whose mother came from Stornoway. The ground floor was made over to shops, one of which sold both drapery and groceries, with tea being a speciality. Later the shop was taken over by Messrs. Thomas Lipton who, coincidentally, made his name and a fortune from his bizarre methods of advertising his tea.

70. This view is of South Beach harbour with Stornoway's No. 3 pier on the left. This was a wooden structure built about 1893 to extend the harbour facilities which could not cope with the hundreds of fishing and other vessels which came into Stornoway during the height of the herring season. Even with the No. 3 wharf, many boats had to ride at anchor in the bay. On the pier can be seen much of the activity which was a common sight in the town until the 1930s. The cargo vessel berthed at the wharf is no doubt taking on barrels of salted herrings for subsequent despatch to Germany, Estonia, Latvia and Lithuania and the free Baltic port of Danzig. At the turn of the century, when the fishing industry was at its busiest, the town's population, normally about 2,000, swelled to many thousands and its streets were filled with many nationalities. No. 3 wharf was demolished a number of years ago and has never been replaced. This part of the harbour was constructed just before the turn of the century and is now used for car-parking.

71. This picture shows the 'Clansman' getting up steam to leave Stornoway Harbour, c. 1900. She was built in 1870 and became a well-known favourite for the route for which she was designed, namely the Glasgow-Stornoway services. She was a very attractive ship with two masts and a clipper bow, figurehead and bowsprit with ornamental carving both at bow and stern. Electric lighting was installed in 1904. She plied her route for forty years until she was broken up in 1910. Leaving Glasgow on Monday mornings, the 'Clansman' sailed north, calling at various ports on the west coast of Scotland, and returning to Glasgow on the following Saturday. The hill seen in the background is Gallows Hill, so called because it was here that, during the period in the 17th century, when the MacLeods ruled Lewis, wrongdoers were committed to the 'pit and gallows'. The remains of a platform and large stones can still be seen on the site where justice was meted out. Fishing wherries can be seen tied up at the pier.

"The Claymore" at Stornoway

W. J. Tolmie, Stornoway.

72. This picture, c. 1910, shows the 'Claymore' which was the sister ship to the 'Clansman'. Built in 1881, her lines generally followed those of the 'Clansman'. She was also on the Glasgow-Stornoway route, leaving Glasgow on Thursday mornings and returning there on the following Wednesday. Carrying both passengers and cargo, the 'Claymore' was a familiar and welcome sight in many west coast ports of call. During the First World War she was camouflaged to elude German submarines. In January 1910 she went ashore on rocks near Pabbay, close to Broadford in Skye, but after repair went back into regular service again. She was sold in 1931 for breaking up. But so highly regarded was the 'Claymore' by all who had sailed in her that the ship-breakers were inundated with requests for souvenirs from the ship. In fact, relics of the ship were sent all over Scotland and England. The wood panelling from the saloon was rescued to be installed in the Municipal Buildings in Oban. The ship's figurehead was also rescued and for many years graced a garden in Forfarshire.

73. The motto on the coat of arms of the old Burgh of Stornoway was: 'God's Providence is our Inheritance.' The 'providence' was the prosperity which derived from the richness of the seas round the Hebrides. The abundance of fish in these waters was recognised as long ago as 1633 by King Charles I. He was interested in buying Lewis to be the main seat of operation of a fishing company set up to exploit the sea's wealth. The scheme, however, fell flat in 1640 and though Charles II tried to revive the plan, lack of capital resulted in failure. Later Lord Seaforth decided to pursue a plan of his own. For its success it needed expert fishermen and he brought Dutch fishing busses to Lewis, with Stornoway as the main port. When a war between Britain and Holland broke out in 1653, the Dutch had to leave Lewis. It was not until about 1850 that fish-curers from the Scottish east coast realised the enormous potential for the herring fishing. In less than a decade Stornoway was one of the major herring ports in Europe. This picture, c. 1900, shows the herring fleet making for deep waters.

74. This picture, c. 1910, shows a crowd gathering on the No. 2 timber-built wharf at Stornoway, more than interested in the high quality large fish just landed. This wharf was replaced by a concrete structure in 1938. The size of the cod and halibut shown here indicates the reason why Stornoway had a lucrative trade in fish exports. These, of course, were the years before the advent of industrial fishing over-fishing which took both mature and young fish from the sea, thus depleting stocks. Most of these fish were caught on fishing lines, many metres long, with hooks attached to them from small strings which were once made from horsehair. The long lines were left 48 hours or more. Cod, in particular, yielded valuable cod-liver oil. Most of the fish were caught less than 3 miles from the shore and so small open boats could be used, most of them equipped with oars. With the advent of the steam trawler in the 1880s, much of the long-line fishing industry declined because the trawlers ripped away the lines and fishermen were forced to lay the lines without marker buoys, and grapple for the lines on the sea bed.

75. This picture shows herring girls gutting herring from a station on the Cromwell Street pier. The white building in the background is the Royal Hotel. The tower-like structure (background left) is the 'Boat House', from which a boatman ferried passengers between the quay and the Castle grounds. The scene shown here was a familiar sight on Stornoway quays until the 1930s. The herring were dumped into a large wooden trough known as a 'farlin'. The job of the herring girls was to gut the herring and throw the fish into tubs, arranged at the back of each pair of gutters, according to the type of fish: smalls, fulls and matties. An expert gutter could gut and grade 60 to 70 herrings a minute. Each barrel was packed by a packer who arranged layers of herring and salt so that the barrel was solid and tight. A barrel could hold between 700 and 1000 herrings depending on size. A packer aimed at filling three barrels an hour. The fingers of the gutters were protected from salt and the sharp gutting knife by cloth bindings tied separately round each finger. Wounds often took a long time to heal.

76. A typical harbour scene, c. 1890. The small boat in the middle is an early type of 'Skaffie', based on boats of Norse origin and unusual in the rake of the stern and curved stem. Later these boats were decked overall. From about 1880 these smaller boats were replaced by the 'Zulu' fishing wherry, of the kind seen in the large boat. The unusual name was derived from the fact that the war in South Africa had just been concluded and the name stuck. These boats had long raked sterns with a keel length of 20m and an overall length of nearly 30m. A contemporary description says: 'It is truly one of the finest sights of modern times to see this great brown pyramid (the sail) coming marching up out of the horizon, and go leaning by you at a tenknot speed, the peak stabbing the sky as it lurches past some seventy feet above the water'. The mast carrying the massive sail was like a large tree, some as much as two feet in diameter at deck level. These boats were eventually replaced by the steam herring drifter.